They Came to Britain

The History of a Multicultural Nation

Philip Page
Heather Newman

Edward Arnold

First published in Great Britain 1985 by
Edward Arnold (Publishers) Ltd, 41 Bedford Square,
London WC1B 3DQ

Edward Arnold (Australia) Pty Ltd, 80 Waverley
Road, Caulfield East, Victoria 3145, Australia

Reprinted 1986

British Library Cataloguing in Publication Data

Page, Philip
    They came to Britain: the history of a multicultural
    nation.
    1. Great Britain——Emigration and
        immigration——History
    I. Title   II. Newman, Heather
      304.8'41   JV7620

    ISBN 0–7131–7380–7

Text set in 11/12pt Times
by Castlefield Press, Moulton, Northampton
Printed and bound at The Bath Press, Avon

Introduction

We are living in a multi-racial and multi-cultural society in Britain today. Many people mistakenly believe that this is something that has only happened recently. Many people believe that an immigrant is somebody with a black or brown skin. This also is untrue.

The purpose of this book is to tell the story of how our society has been built up, over centuries and even longer, of people from outside the British Isles and to look at the contribution they have made. It is an introduction to a wide and fascinating part of our history which has tended to be neglected. Because its theme is the historical background to immigration, it is not intended to deal in detail with the various cultures and lifestyles of different groups, nor can it examine in depth the many problems encountered by those groups. There are already many excellent publications covering those aspects and it is hoped that this book will be used in conjunction with them.

Philip Page
Heather Newman

Acknowledgements
The authors would like to thank the following for their help in producing this book:
Carmen Beckford MBE; PC Vic Brookes; the Commission for Racial Equality; Mr A. Dungarwalla and family; Mrs R. Eugene and family; Yasin Khan; the National Association for Multi-Racial Education; Father Pawet Przybylski; Saltley Action Centre; Saltley Local History Project; Julian Saunders; Zyta Szulejewska; Leah Thorn; John Tyrell and the Multi-cultural Resource Unit, Bordesley Centre, Birmingham, and the staff and pupils of Hodge Hill Girls' School, Birmingham.

The Publishers would like to thank the following for their permission to reproduce copyright illustrations:
Copyright reserved. Reproduced by gracious permission of Her Majesty Queen Elizabeth II p. 26r; Cambridge University Collection: Crown Copyright p. 91; Department of the Environment: Crown Copyright pp. 19b, 201 & 21r; Scottish Development Department: Crown Copyright p. 211; The Mansell Collection Ltd. pp. 81, 11, 12, 14, 24b, 32t, & b & 46t; Kents Cavern Ltd. p. 8r; British Museum pp. 9r & 201 inset; Cambridge University Collection p. 10; B.B.C. Hulton Picture Library pp. 18, 23, 31, 33bl,34, 38 & 42b; Michael Holford Library p. 19t; A. F. Kersting pp. 20r & 40; Reece Winstone p. 261; Birmingham Post & Mail p. 28; The Borough of Trafford: Stretford Central Library p. 33tr; Popperfoto p. 361 & r; The United Nations High Commission for Refugees/K. Gaugher p. 39; Topham Picture Library p. 42t; Island Records Ltd. p.46b; The photographs on pp. 6, 35b & t & 45 were supplied by the author. Despite every effort the publishers have failed to trace the copyright holders of the pictures on pages 22 & 27.

Contents

1 'Typically British'

We all have our own idea of what people from other countries are like. We see them in films and on television. We meet them if we go abroad and we see them when they visit Britain. There are pictures of them in newspapers and books and we learn about them at school. We know, of course, that no two people are exactly alike. But we do think that it is often possible to tell where people come from simply by looking at them.

Look at the pictures below. Which would you say showed:
a) 'typical Americans'
b) 'typical French'
c) 'typical Saudi-Arabians'
d) 'typical Japanese'?

It's quite easy isn't it? It's easy because these are simple cartoons and are not meant to show individual people. We know that not all Americans are white and wear cowboy hats. We know that not all Japanese are small and wear glasses.

Have you ever wondered how people in other countries see us, the British? Look at the cartoon above. This is what many people abroad think a 'typical Briton' looks like. Do you think this is accurate?

What is wrong with the picture? There *are* British people who *do* look like this. However, we know that there are millions more who do not.

Would you say that the picture shows a Welshman, a Scot, somebody from Northern Ireland or an Englishman? You would probably say that the man is English. To many people in other countries, somebody or something that is 'typically British' is the same as being English.

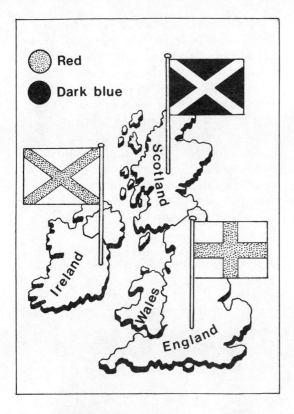

Red

Dark blue

Scotland

Ireland

Wales

England

Welsh girl
from Llanberis

Irish
dancer

Scottish
kilt

However, Britain is not just England. We only have to look at our national flag, the 'Union Jack' to remember this. It is made up of three crosses: those of St. George of England, St. Andrew of Scotland and St. Patrick of Ireland. The Union Jack reminds us that the British are a mixture of people who live in what were once different countries in the British Isles.

England and Wales were joined together in 1536 in the reign of King Henry VIII. After the death of Queen Elizabeth I in 1603, King James of Scotland became King of England as well as Scotland. Ireland was joined to Britain in 1801, although Eire (Southern Ireland) left in the 1920s.

So is there such a thing as a 'typical British' person? The answer must surely be 'no'. The man in the bowler hat carrying the rolled umbrella is no more typical than you are, or anybody else reading this book in your class or in any other part of Britain.

The fact is that the British are a mixture of different peoples. They always have been and they still are today. You only have to look around you to realise this. In schools, factories and offices there are people with different names and different coloured skin.

In the streets there are restaurants and shops which sell different types of food and clothes. There are different places where people go to worship: churches, synagogues, chapels, mosques and gurdwaras. All the people who have these different names, colours, clothes, customs and religions are alike in one way at least – they can all be British.

The picture on the left shows national costumes from Wales, Scotland and Ireland which can still be seen to this day. They are a reminder of how varied British culture has always been. How dull it would be if Britain did not have its many variations in language, dialect, food, music and other things!

5

Look at this photograph of a group of schoolgirls. One thing they have in common is that they all go to the same school in Birmingham. Yet at some time in the past, all their families came from countries outside England. They have another thing in common – they are all British.

All our **ancestors** came to Britain from somewhere else. Some only came a few years ago, but others came hundreds of years ago. Even the English, Scots, Welsh and Irish did not originally come from the British Isles. At one time all their **ancestors** were **immigrants**. Yet we often think of **immigrants** as being people who have only recently come to this country.

For thousands of years people have been coming to what we now call the British Isles. But who were all these people? When and why did they come? What pieces of our national jigsaw did they bring with them?

To try to answer these questions we shall be looking at some of these groups of people: those who came to fight and conquer; those who were attracted or encouraged to settle here; and those who came looking for a new home because they had been forced to leave their own countries. Their stories are our history: they are our **ancestors**.

The time-chart on the next page shows when the people mentioned in this book came to this country.

From left to right: Margaret Kudryl, Lubna Malik, Jane Llewellyn, Louise Reilly, Sui Mun Chau, Sofia Konnarides, Lisa Macdonald, Corinne Allen.

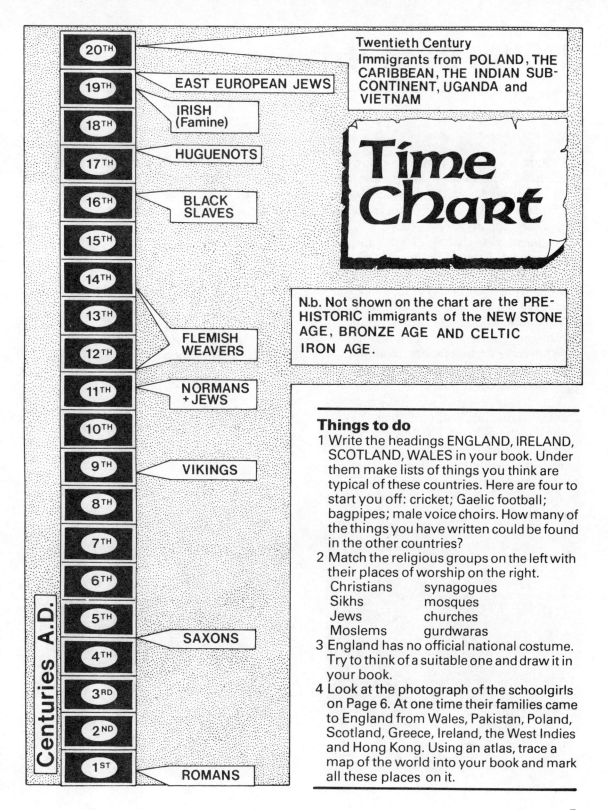

Centuries A.D.

Century	Immigrants
20TH	
19TH	EAST EUROPEAN JEWS
18TH	IRISH (Famine)
17TH	HUGUENOTS
16TH	BLACK SLAVES
15TH	
14TH	
13TH	
12TH	FLEMISH WEAVERS
11TH	NORMANS + JEWS
10TH	
9TH	VIKINGS
8TH	
7TH	
6TH	
5TH	
4TH	SAXONS
3RD	
2ND	
1ST	ROMANS

Twentieth Century
Immigrants from POLAND, THE CARIBBEAN, THE INDIAN SUB-CONTINENT, UGANDA and VIETNAM

Time Chart

N.b. Not shown on the chart are the PRE-HISTORIC immigrants of the NEW STONE AGE, BRONZE AGE AND CELTIC IRON AGE.

Things to do

1 Write the headings ENGLAND, IRELAND, SCOTLAND, WALES in your book. Under them make lists of things you think are typical of these countries. Here are four to start you off: cricket; Gaelic football; bagpipes; male voice choirs. How many of the things you have written could be found in the other countries?

2 Match the religious groups on the left with their places of worship on the right.

  Christians   synagogues
  Sikhs   mosques
  Jews   churches
  Moslems   gurdwaras

3 England has no official national costume. Try to think of a suitable one and draw it in your book.

4 Look at the photograph of the schoolgirls on Page 6. At one time their families came to England from Wales, Pakistan, Poland, Scotland, Greece, Ireland, the West Indies and Hong Kong. Using an atlas, trace a map of the world into your book and mark all these places on it.

2 The First Britons

If Britain is a nation of **immigrants**, who came first? Who were the first people to live in the British Isles and what were they like? To find the answers to these questions we have to ask the **archaeologists**.

Archaeologists try to find out about the past by looking for things people leave behind. We cannot find out about the first Britons from their books or letters because they did not know how to read or write. We call the time when these people lived 'prehistoric', or *before* written history.

What have **archaeologists** found out about the first Britons? Look at these clues that the prehistoric people left.

This is part of a skull which is over 250 000 years old! It was found at Swanscombe in Kent. Experts have discovered that it belonged to a human being, not an animal, so that person was one of the first to live in this country. From bones such as this it is possible to guess what the people looked like.

These are some of the things that the first people in Britain made. Most things were made of stone so we call this time the Old Stone Age. These people hunted and gathered their food: they did not know how to farm.

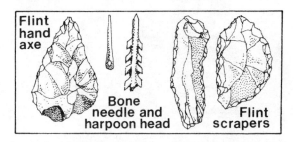

In parts of Britain, caves have been found where some of these people lived. The fires they lit left blackened stones. The bones of the animals they ate have been found in the caves.

This is Kents Cavern in Torquay in Devon where remains of Old Stone Age people have been found.

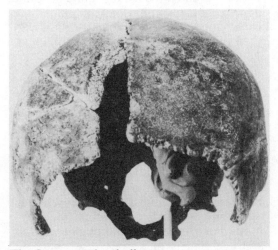

The Swanscombe skull

Kents Cavern, Torquay

About 5000 BC some new people began to arrive in Britain. They did not get their food just by hunting and gathering. They knew how to farm: they could keep animals and grow crops. This meant that they did not have to be on the move all the time looking for food. So they stayed in one place and built more comfortable homes.

One of the first places where these early farmers lived was Windmill Hill in Wiltshire. This is what it looks like today. Can you see the rings of ditches they dug? **Archaeologists** think that the farmers kept their animals in the middle of these rings. The bones of cattle, sheep, pigs and goats have been found here.

Windmill Hill

These people still made things from stone, but because of the change from hunting to farming, we call their time the New Stone Age. These people also brought pottery to Britain.

The skeleton opposite is of a man who lived in Southern Britain about 2000 BC. He belonged to a new group of immigrants whom we call the Beaker People. They brought with them things made of metal. Gold jewellery and copper daggers have been found in their tombs. Copper is a soft metal, but they soon found that if they mixed it with a small amount of tin they got a harder metal. This mixture is called bronze.

From about 2000 BC to about 600 BC bronze was the main metal used in Britain.

That is why that period is called the Bronze Age. The Bronze Age people brought the wheel and weaving to this country. They also finished building Stonehenge, putting up the great stones we can see there today.

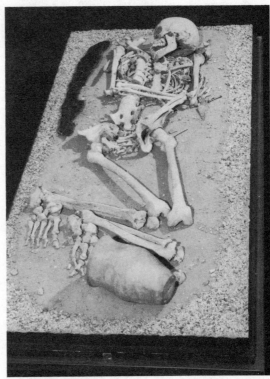

A 'Beaker' burial

Things to do

1 Use the information on Page 8 to complete the following sentences:
Old Stone Age people got their _____ by hunting and gathering. Some of them lived in _____ like Kent's Cavern. They made things from stone, wood and _____.
2 What evidence is there that the Old Stone Age people wore clothes? What do you think they were made of?
3 Look at the picture of the skeleton. How do you think the Beaker People got their name?
4 Can you think of some ways in which farming made life easier for these people than hunting and gathering their food?

a) The Celts

In parts of Ireland, Scotland, Wales and Cornwall today there are people whose **ancestors** were the Celts. The first Celts started to come to Britain from Central Europe in about 600 BC. The last to arrive did not come until about 500 years later.

The Celts brought with them a new metal: iron. Iron is much stronger than bronze and can be made sharper. The time of the Celts in Britain is known as the Iron Age.

The Celts belonged to different tribes such as the Silures, who lived in what is now South Wales, and the Iceni, who lived in what is now Norfolk. It seems that many of the tribes often fought against each other. **Archaeologists** have found Celtic forts. They have also found helmets, shields and swords, such as the ones opposite, which once belonged to Celtic warriors.

The remains of the farmhouses and fields left by the Celtic farmers can still be seen in parts of Britain today. But the most spectacular remains are those of the places the Celts built to protect thmselves against attacks by other Celts. Can you spot the defensive ditches and the entrance to this Iron Age hill-fort at Hambledon Hill in Dorset?

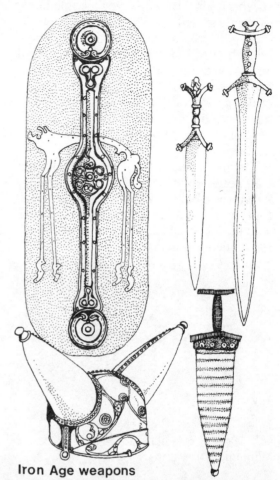

Iron Age weapons

10

We know a lot about the Celts, not only from the things they made and built, but also from what was written about them. The writers were Romans who came to Britain and fought the Celts. This is what one Roman, Julius Caesar, wrote about the British Celts:

The population is exceedingly large, the ground thickly studded with homesteads...and the cattle very numerous. For money they use either bronze, or gold coins, or iron ingots (bars) ...Hares, fowl and geese they think it is unlawful to eat, but rear them for pleasure...

Most of the tribes...do not grow corn, but live on milk and meat, and wear skins. All the Britons dye their bodies with woad, which produces a blue colour and this gives them a more terrifying appearance in battle. They wear their hair long, and shave the whole of their bodies except the head and upper lip.

In chariot fighting, the Britons begin by driving all over the field hurling javelins...Then...they jump down from the chariots and engage (fight) on foot....by daily training and practice they attain such proficiency (skill) that even on a steep incline they are able to control the horses at full gallop, and to check (stop) and turn them in a moment.

Things to do

1 Use Julius Caesar's description and the pictures on Page 10 to draw and colour a picture of a Celtic warrior with his helmet, shield and weapons.

2 Look at the picture of Hambledon Hill. What difficulties would attackers have faced if they tried to get into this hill-fort?

3 Read Julius Caesar's description of the Celts. He was writing about his enemy and wanted his readers to think that they were fierce fighters. How does he create this impression?

4 The Celts were very fond of horses. They carved a huge picture of one on a hillside at Uffington in Oxfordshire. Trace these shapes on to a piece of paper, cut them out and fit them together to make a picture of the White Horse of Uffington. Colour the dark parts green.

3 The Conquerors

Look closely at the faces of these men. Soldiers like them invaded this country and conquered it for their leaders. Since the time of the Celts, this has happened four times.

Can you identify the conquerors? See if you can match the correct picture to these descriptions:

1 A Roman soldier (copied from a carving on Trajan's Column in Rome)
2 A Saxon warrior (copied from an 8th-century carving)
3 A Viking warrior (copied from a carving in Sweden)
4 A Norman knight (copied from the Bayeux Tapestry)

We know that each of the conquerors had to fight to get control of this country and that they defeated the people who were here before them. Once they had done this, their own people came to settle down in Britain. In this chapter we shall look at their reasons for coming here and the changes they made once they were in control.

a) The Romans

This is the head of a statue of the Roman Emperor Claudius. In AD 43, 87 years after Julius Caesar raided Britain, Claudius sent an army of about 40 000 men to conquer this country. Why did he do this?

Claudius became emperor in AD 41. The army in Rome chose him after they had killed Caligula, the previous emperor. Claudius gave them money and tried to keep their support – he did not want them to kill him! Perhaps he wanted to win a great victory for the army and himself. Perhaps he wanted to impress the Roman people. We do not know the answer for certain.

If he did want a victory, why did he choose Britain? Was this country worth the trouble and expense of invading? Let us look at what two Roman writers said about Britain at the time.

Both these are Roman versions of why the Romans invaded, but Tacitus also gives us a different point of view. He wrote what a Caledonian (Scottish) chief called Calgacus said about the Romans.

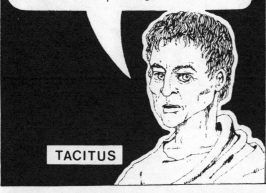

The climate is objectionable, with its frequent rains and mists, but there is no extreme cold...the soil can bear all produce (crops), and it is fertile...Britain yields gold, silver and other metals to make it worth conquering.

TACITUS

They are unique in being as violently tempted to attack the poor as the wealthy. Robbery, butchery...the liars call Empire; they create a desolation and call it peace... Here before us is their general, here his army; behind are the tribute (taxes), the mines and all the other whips to scourge (beat) slaves.

CALGACUS

Claudius' sole (only) campaign was of no great importance... (Britain's) conquest had not been attempted since Julius Caesar's day; and the Britons were now threatening vengeance (revenge) because the Senate (Rome's government) refused to extradite (send back) certain deserters who had landed in Gaul (France) during Caligula's reign.

SUETONIUS

Things to do

1 Using the evidence you have read, make a list of the possible reasons for the Roman invasion of AD 43.
2 Claudius and Calgacus would not have chosen the same reason to explain why the Romans came to conquer Britain. Which reasons do you think each of them would have given? Give reasons for your choice.

b) The Anglo-Saxons

After the invasion of AD 43, Britain became part of the Roman Empire. However, about 300 years later the Roman Empire itself was attacked by people who lived outside it. The Romans called these people 'barbarians', and tried to fight them off.

The soldiers were taken from Britain to defend Rome in the early 5th century. Without them, the British leaders found it difficult to stop the barbarians attacking this country.

In AD 410 the Roman Emperor wrote to the Britons to tell them Rome could not give them any more help. About 30 years later, the Britons made a last, desperate attempt to get help from Rome. They wrote a letter saying

> . . . the barbarians drive us to the sea, the sea drives us to the barbarians; between these two means of death we are either killed or drowned.

The letter was never answered.

This carving of Saxon warriors is on the side of a casket which was made in the 8th century AD

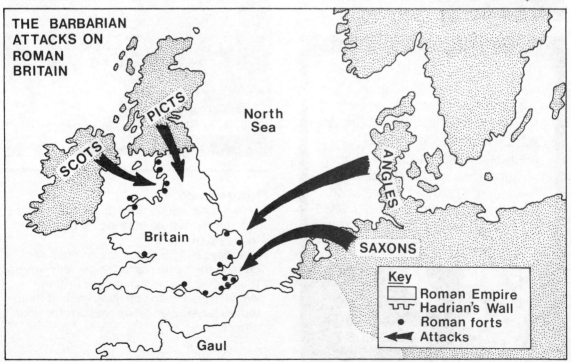

THE BARBARIAN ATTACKS ON ROMAN BRITAIN

PICTS

North Sea

SCOTS

ANGLES

Britain

SAXONS

Key
Roman Empire
Hadrian's Wall
Roman forts
Attacks

Gaul

14

What happened next was described by a Saxon monk about 300 years later. His name was Bede. In AD 731 he wrote one of the first history books in this country. He told what Vortigern, a British leader, did to stop the attacks of the Picts and the terrible results of his decision:

...the Angles or Saxons came to Britain at the invitation of King Vortigern in three longships, and were granted lands in the eastern part of the island on condition that they protected the country: nevertheless, their real intention was to subdue (conquer) it. They engaged the enemy advancing from the north, and having defeated them, sent back news of their success to their homeland, adding that the country was fertile and the Britons cowardly. Whereupon a larger fleet came over with a great body of warriors.

...It was not long before such hordes of these alien people vied (competed) together to crowd into the island that the natives who had invited them began to live in terror... these heathen (non-Christian) conquerors devastated the...cities and countryside...buildings were razed (destroyed), priests were slain at the altar; bishops and people alike... were destroyed with fire and sword. ...A few wretched survivors captured in the hills were butchered...and others, desperate with hunger, came out and surrendered... although they were doomed to lifelong slavery even if they escaped instant massacre.

BEDE

Things to do

1 Why could the Romans not send any help to Britain in the early 5th century?
2 Look at the map and at what Bede wrote. Whom do you think Vortigern believed was the greater threat to Britain: the Picts or the Anglo-Saxons? Give a reason for your answer.
3 What two reasons does Bede give for the Anglo-Saxons' decision to conquer Britain?
4 Try making a quill pen like Bede's by sharpening the end of a feather. Use it to write in your own words what happened to the Britons.

c) The Vikings

Bede lived in a monastery at Jarrow in the Saxon kingdom of Northumbria. In AD 794, 59 years after his death, that monastery was attacked and robbed by raiders from across the North Sea.

The raiders were Vikings. They had made their first raid the year before when they destroyed the church on the island of Lindisfarne. A monk called Alcuin wrote a letter from Europe, where he was living, to the King of Northumbria. In it he described what had happened.

Year after year, the Vikings raided the coasts of the British Isles. Usually they did not stay for long. Then, in AD 851, they changed their hit-and-run tactics. The *Anglo-Saxon Chronicle*, a sort of diary started by monks in the late 9th century, says:

> The heathen men [Vikings] stayed over the winter, and that year [851] three hundred and fifty ships came to the mouth of the Thames; they ruined Canterbury, put to flight . . . the Mercian king with his troops. . . .

Lo, it is nearly 350 years that we and our fathers have inhabited this most lovely land, and never before has such a terror appeared in Britain as we have suffered from a pagan (non-Christian) race, nor was it thought that such an inroad (attack) from the sea could be made.

Behold, the church of St. Cuthbert spattered with the blood of the priests of God, despoiled (robbed) of all its ornaments, a place more venerable (respected) than all in Britain is given as a prey (victim) to pagan peoples.

What Alcuin wrote

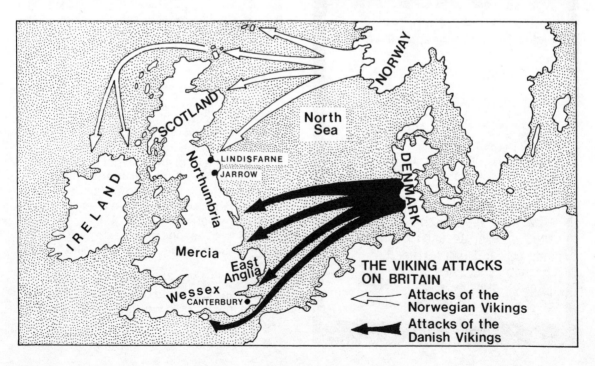

THE VIKING ATTACKS ON BRITAIN

← Attacks of the Norwegian Vikings

◀ Attacks of the Danish Vikings

16

In AD 866, 'a great heathen force came into the English land, and they took winter quarters in East Anglia.' This sentence from the *Anglo-Saxon Chronicle* tells of another change: this time the Vikings had come to stay!

What brought the Vikings to Britain? Why did they decide to remain here and settle the land with their families? The Norwegians were looking for new lands in which to live. Their own homeland was becoming overcrowded. There was a shortage of good farmland as much of Norway was, and still is, mountainous and heavily forested. It was the Norwegians who settled in Scotland and sailed across the North Atlantic to Iceland, Greenland and North America.

The Danes did not suffer from a shortage of land: they were seeking **plunder** and profit from their raids. They sailed as far south as the Mediterranean and North Africa in search of them. Saxon England was rich and its people were not strong enough to keep the Danes away. It was an easy step for them to stay for longer and longer periods of time before deciding to settle here permanently.

However, the Saxons did fight back. In AD 878 King Alfred the Great of Wessex halted the Danish advance. They could go no further than the 'Danelaw' in the eastern part of England. Alfred's successors began to re-conquer the Danelaw. Then, in 1014, King Ethelred the Unready fled across the Channel leaving England at the mercy of the Danes. Three years later, a Dane called Canute became King of England.

Things to do

1 Trace the map on Page 16 into your book. Use different colours to show where the Vikings came from and where they attacked.
2 Churches and monasteries were easy targets for the early Viking raiders. Why do you think this was? What could be stolen from them?
3 Explain how and why the Vikings changed their tactics in the mid-9th century.
4 Imagine that you are the Viking raider in the picture above. Describe the scene around you and what your crew plans to do on this raid.

This picture from the Bayeux Tapestry shows the death of Harold; the writing says 'King Harold has been killed'

d) The Normans

In 1066 the last conquest of Britain took place. Duke William of Normandy (which is now part of France) invaded England and killed King Harold at the Battle of Hastings on 14 October. On Christmas Day 1066 William was crowned King of England in Westminster Abbey in London.

Why did William invade? On 5 January 1066, King Edward the Confessor of England died. He had no children and Harold, the most powerful of the English nobles, made himself king. He was crowned the next day. Duke William said that King Edward had promised him that he would be the next king. He also said that, during a visit to Normandy, Harold had sworn an oath (made a solemn promise) that he would help William to become king of England. William invaded because he said Harold had broken his promise.

How do we know about this broken promise? Was such a promise ever made?

Make up your own mind after you have looked at the evidence.

Evidence A: *The Anglo-Saxon Chronicle*, which was still being written, does not mention the oath. It does not even say that Harold ever went to Normandy. It does say that King Edward, when he was dying, 'committed [gave] the kingdom to one high in rank, Harold himself. . . .'

Evidence B: The Bayeux Tapestry was embroidered for the Normans soon after 1066. It tells the story of the Conquest in a series of pictures. The picture on the next page shows William seated at the left. On the right is Harold. They are in Normandy and Harold is touching two boxes in which are the bones of saints. The writing (in Latin) says 'Where Harold made an oath to Duke William.'

Evidence C: A Norman called William of Poitiers wrote a book telling the story of the Conquest. He was alive at the time but did

The Bayeux Tapestry shows Harold taking the oath

not take part in the invasion. This is part of what he wrote:

> Edward, King of the English, loved William as much as if the duke had been his brother or his son, and he had long appointed [chosen] him as his heir . . . In order to confirm his promise by oath, he sent Harold to William, Harold, the wealthiest of all his subjects, the most powerful and the most highly honoured . . .
>
> . . . Harold swore an oath of fidelity [loyalty] to William. A number of extremely famous men who are not given to lying, whose word can be trusted and who . . . were present and witnessed the event, have told me how, freely and distinctly [clearly] . . . Harold [said] that after Edward's death he would do everything in his power . . . to confirm William in his succession to the throne.

To protect themselves in a conquered land, the Normans built motte and bailey castles like this one at Berkhamstead, Hertfordshire

Things to do

1 From the evidence you have seen and read, do you think there was an oath or not? Give reasons for your opinion.
2 Divide a page in your book into six equal sections. In them, draw and label your own comic strip to tell the story of the events of the quarrel between William and Harold from the point of view of *either* the Saxons or the Normans.

19

c) The Legacy of the Conquerors

Is there anything left today to remind us of the conquerors, or is all that remains of them only to be found in museums or History books? To believe that they made no mark on the landscape of Britain or on our lives is a mistake – signs of what they left behind can be found all around us.

The Romans

If you travel along the A5 road north from St. Albans, you will be following the route of an old Roman road. You might live in one of the old Roman towns such as Lindum (Lincoln), Londinium (London), Eboracum (York) or Glevum (Gloucester).

Latin, the Romans' language, is still used in medicine, science and the law. When we use abbreviations, like 'N.B.' and 'e.g.', we are using Latin. Roman lettering can be seen on many **inscriptions** on public buildings.

The remains of Roman buildings are to be found in many places – the lighthouse at Dover; the villa at Chedworth; the palace at Fishbourne; the fort at Portchester and, of course, the great wall built on the Emperor Hadrian's orders across the north of England.

Finally, do you recognise the figure on the Roman coin?

Hadrian's Wall

The Anglo-Saxons

What has a sheriff got to do with the Saxons? The answer is that his name comes from the title of a Saxon official: the 'shire reeve'. There may not be many Saxon buildings left to remind us of them, but the English we speak today is based on the language of the Anglo-Saxons.

The days of the week are named after their gods and goddesses. For example, Tuesday is named after Tiew (the god of war) and Wednesday after Woden (the father of the gods). The ending of many place-names are also Saxon, like -ton, -ham, -den, and -hurst.

It was during the time of the Saxons that England became Christian again. The name 'England' comes from 'Angle-land', and can you guess which counties are named after the North Folk and the East Saxons?

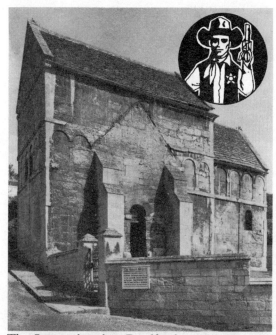

The Saxon church at Bradford-on-Avon

The Vikings

Every year, on the last Tuesday in January, the people of Lerwick in the Shetland Islands dress up as Vikings and ceremonially burn a copy of a Viking longboat. This festival of Up-Helly-Aa is a modern one, but it celebrates the fact that the Vikings once lived in those islands.

Further south there are more reminders of the Vikings. Many towns have Viking name endings like -by, -thorp(e), -thwaite and -toft. These are mainly in the north and east of England. Page 17 will give you a clue as to why this is. Other Viking sites have been found at York, Dublin and the Isle of Man.

When you say 'sky', 'die', 'berserk', 'get' or 'egg', you are using Viking words.

Jarlshof, a Viking settlement on the Shetlands

The Normans

Signs of the Normans can be seen all over England. The great stone castle keeps they built to protect themselves can be found at Rochester in Kent, Richmond in Yorkshire and in London, where the White Tower is the keep of the Tower of London.

There may not be a Norman castle near to where you live, but there will probably be a church. Many old churches still have parts dating back to Norman times. Rounded arches over doors and windows are a sign of Norman architecture.

The Normans brought their own language with them: Norman French. Words like 'parliament' and 'government' came with these conquerors, as did the names of cooked meats such as pork (*porc*), beef (*boeuf*) and mutton (*mouton*).

Rochester Castle

Things to do

1 Use an atlas or a map of England to find ten places with Saxon name endings and ten with Viking name endings.
(Remember where to look for the Viking ones.)
2 Make up a sentence including four Viking words.
3 Make a list of the names and other words in this square (they are all from this chapter) and say whether they are Roman, Saxon, Viking or Norman.

Z	E	G	G	T	H	Q	S	K	Y
P	A	R	L	I	A	M	E	N	T
O	X	M	E	E	P	W	G	L	B
R	B	I	V	W	U	F	M	L	A
K	E	W	U	J	K	D	V	I	O
Q	R	S	M	U	T	T	O	N	W
E	S	S	E	X	J	G	R	D	O
K	E	F	G	Y	Z	X	P	U	D
U	R	W	D	G	Y	I	N	M	E
J	K	N	O	R	F	O	L	K	N

4 The Settlers

The Normans were the last people to succeed in conquering this country. There have been others who have tried since then (Philip II of Spain in 1588, Napoleon in 1805 and Hitler in 1940) but they have all failed. From 1066 to the present day, all the people who have come here have done so peacefully.

Over the centuries many different groups of people from other countries have been attracted to Britain and have chosen to come here to start a new life for themselves. In this chapter we shall be looking at some of them to see what made them decide to settle here and make Britain their home.

The Norman Conquest meant that England became more closely linked to the Continent than at any time since Britain had been part of the Roman Empire. With William came not only the soldiers and Norman lords, but also architects, builders, clergymen and craftsmen and their families.

When later kings and queens married people from other countries, these people brought their own courtiers and servants with them. This happened when King Henry II married Eleanor of Aquitaine in 1152, and when Mary I married Philip of Spain in 1554. It happened in Scotland when King James V married Mary of Guise in 1538. Their daughter, Mary Queen of Scots, spent her childhood in France.

However, most of the foreign settlers had nothing to do with the royal court, although some were encouraged by kings to bring their skills and knowledge across the Channel. In 1113 King Henry I invited the weavers of Flanders to come to England. Flemish weavers were among the best in Europe. In 1337 Edward III followed Henry's example. In that year he issued an

A 14th-century drawing of Flemish wool merchants

invitation to foreign weavers saying that:

> All the cloth workers of strange lands of whatsoever country they be, which will come to England . . . shall come safely and securely, and shall be in the King's protection. . . .

Other craftsmen besides weavers came to settle here. In 1440 King Henry VI decided to tax all '**aliens**' in England and so, for the first time, a list was made of all foreigners living and working here. It did not include merchants or noblemen's servants, but it showed that foreigners numbered about 1 per cent of the population (about 16 000 in all), and that they mainly lived in the towns. Many English people thought that there were far more of them here than the official number.

This list, or census, gives us an idea of who these immigrant settlers were and what they did. There were the 'Doche' (Dutch, Flemish and Germans) who were weavers,

22

A painting of George Gisze by Hans Holbein

merchants brought in iron, and Norwegians imported tar for shipbuilding. French merchants organised the wine trade with France.

Perhaps the most powerful and well-known group of foreign merchants were those who belonged to the Hanse. The Hanse was a trading organisation of North German towns along the coast of the Baltic Sea. In London their merchants lived in a district known as the 'Steelyard', where they had their offices, warehouses and churches. They lent the English kings money, and in return were given special trading and taxation privileges. The picture on the left is of one of these merchants, Georg Gisze. It was painted in 1532 by Hans Holbein, who was himself a German and court painter to King Henry VIII.

Today people come to live in Britain for a variety of reasons, although the trend in recent years has been for more people to leave this country to live abroad each year. Some only stay here for a short time before returning to their homeland. Such people include students who come here to study, or others who are training for a job or who have been sent here to work for a branch of a foreign-owned business. Most of these people stay for only a few years, but some decide to make Britain their home and become British citizens.

goldsmiths, tailors, leather-makers and brewers. The 'Frenssh', who seemed to have settled mainly in Kent, were weavers and brewers as well but were also builders, millers and smiths. The 'Yrish' and 'Scotch' were often herdsmen, employed in driving sheep and cattle to the towns to market and also from winter to summer pastures. A number of doctors came from Mediterranean lands.

As well as craftsmen, there were foreign merchants living in England. For many of them this was not their permanent home. But some stayed here, as did some of their servants, workers, clerks and of course their families. Medieval England traded with many parts of Europe and much of this trade was organised by foreign merchants (often much to the annoyance of English people).

The Genoese and Venetians, from what is now Italy, ran the trade in spices and silks from the Mediterranean. Spanish

Things to do

1 Match this list of settlers with their reasons for coming to Britain.

Students	were invited to come.
Flemish weavers	come because of trade
Merchants	came with kings and queens.
Courtiers	come to study here.

2 Which of the settlers you have read about were invited to come, and why?

3 Some of the settlers had no choice about coming. Who were they and why did they come?

a) The Jews

The first Jewish settlers came to England after the Norman Conquest of 1066. They had worked for the Normans as clerks and bankers and came with them to live in towns such as London, Lincoln, York, Norwich and Bristol.

England was a Christian country and the church was very powerful. The Christian church did not like the Jews and they were treated very differently from the rest of the people in this country.

One of the few ways in which they were allowed to make a living was by lending money at interest (charging a fee to the person who borrowed it). The church called this usury and said that it was sinful.

However, this did not stop kings and churchmen borrowing from the Jewish moneylenders to pay their armies and build their castles and cathedrals.

The most famous of the Jewish moneylenders in the Middle Ages was Aaron of Lincoln. When he died in 1185, among the people who still owed him money were the King of Scotland, five earls, one archbishop, two bishops, the towns of Winchester and Southampton and nine abbeys including St Albans and Rievaulx.

Anti-Jewish attitudes

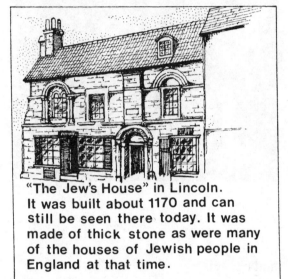

"The Jew's House" in Lincoln. It was built about 1170 and can still be seen there today. It was made of thick stone as were many of the houses of Jewish people in England at that time.

A cartoon on the Jews of Norwich drawn in 1290 during the **persecution** in the reign of Edward I

After Aaron's death, King Henry II took all his treasure. He sent it to France to pay for his war against the French. However, the ship carrying it across the Channel sank in a storm so Henry never got to use it.

The Jews were very important in England in the Middle Ages as bankers and moneylenders. But they were unpopular as many of the English people were suspicious of them. In particular, they did not understand the Jewish religion and Jewish customs. They were ready to believe stories that Jews killed Christian children and drained the blood from their bodies to celebrate the Feast of the Passover.

Below is part of a ballad about 'Little Sir Hugh' who was killed in Lincoln in 1255. It was said that the Jews killed him, although this was never proved. The ballad tells how Hugh was invited into a Jewish house by a lady to fetch a ball he had kicked in there.

In the violence and anti-Jewish riots that followed Hugh's death, 18 people lost their lives.

> She took him by the milk-white hand
> Led him to the hall,
> Till they came to a stone chamber
> Where no-one could heed him call.
>
> She sat him on a golden chair
> She gave him sugars three.
> She lay him on a dressing board
> And stabbed him by degree.
>
> Out came the thick, thick blood,
> Out came the thin.
> Out came the bonny heart's blood
> Till there was none within.
>
> She took him by the yellow hair
> And also by the feet.
> She threw him in the old draw-wall
> Fifty fathoms deep.

The Jews were very useful to the English kings (so much so that in 1254 King Henry III said that they could not leave the country). However, by 1290 they had run out of money to lend and King Edward I

King Edward 1

passed a law expelling the Jews from England. Most left but some became Christians so that they could stay. Some of these probably continued to worship in their own way in secret.

In the mid-17th century, Oliver Cromwell and then King Charles II said that the Jews could return to live in this country and worship openly. Soon there were about 4000 Jews in England and this number doubled in the next hundred years. By 1850 the figure had increased to nearly 35 000, less than 1 per cent of the total population. Among them were Rothschild the banker and Benjamin Disraeli, who became Prime Minister in 1868 and again in the 1870s.

Things to do

1 In your own words, describe why and how the Jews were badly treated in England in the Middle Ages.
2 Why do you think that many Jews built stone houses when most people at the time lived in wooden houses?
3 How did the writer of the ballad suggest that Hugh was killed in a Jewish house?
4 Why did Edward I expel the Jews from England? What reasons might he have given and how truthful do you think they would have been?
5 Discuss with your teacher and the rest of the class whether you think that the cartoon on the Jews of Norwich is fair or unfair.

b) Black Settlers

In the churchyard at Henbury near Bristol is this unusual grave. In it lies the body of a young black slave who spent the last years of his life in Britain.

The first black settlers did not come to this country by choice. Like Scipio, they were slaves who were brought here by force.

The English joined in the slave trade in the 16th century in the reign of Queen Elizabeth I. As the trade grew, so the number of black people who were brought to Britain increased. Many of them became servants.

By the middle of the 18th century there were about 20 000 black people in this country. A lot were servants; some were poor workers or beggars, but a few became famous. Bill Richmond and Tom Molyneux were well-known boxers and Ignatius Sancho was a popular author.

In 1807 Parliament passed an act banning the slave trade. Slaves throughout the British Empire were freed in 1833. Partly as a result of this, the number of black people in Britain began to decline in the 19th century. Some went to the West Indies as free labourers; some emigrated to Sierra Leone in Africa; most intermarried with white British people.

During the 19th century many black people served in Britain's armed forces. Three of them were awarded the Victoria Cross for bravery. Samuel Hodge won his in 1867 and William Gordon of the same West Indian Regiment won his in 1892. In 1857, during the Indian Mutiny, William Hall of Peel's Naval Brigade was awarded the VC.

In the same year Mary Seacole returned from the Crimean War against Russia. Like Florence Nightingale, she had gone to the Crimea as a nurse. Mary came from Jamaica but spent the last years of her life in England where she died in 1881.

During the two world wars of 1914-18 and 1939-45, thousands of black soldiers, sailors and airmen fought for Britain. When the wars ended many of them, like Mary Seacole, chose to stay and live in Britain.

A drummer in the Rifle Brigade, 1815

In June 1948 a group of 492 Jamaicans came to Britain on the *Empire Windrush*. They were the first of a new generation of black settlers who were encouraged to come to Britain to work. After the Second World War there were plenty of jobs in Britain. Many black people were recruited

26

The *Empire Windrush* arriving in Britain

to fill vacancies for organisations such as London Transport and the new National Health Service.

Their numbers increased after 1952 when the United States restricted immigration from the Caribbean. Britain offered opportunities for work and study and these were two of the main reasons why black people came here.

Carmen Beckford and Mrs Eugene both came from the Caribbean. They describe why and how they came to Britain:

Carmen Beckford: 'I was born in Jamaica and lived in the capital, Kingston, before coming to this country. My father was a police inspector: one of the first black men to be appointed to that rank there. He wanted his children to do well and travel and I wanted to be a nurse. I came to train in Middlesex where a schoolfriend was already training.

I arrived in England on board the *Cavina* on May 23rd 1950. Standing on the dock I thought England looked rather bleak and I was amazed to see white men doing menial jobs. I took a train to London and a taxi to the hospital. This used up a lot of my money!

I qualified as a state Registered Nurse in 1953 and went on to become a midwife. I took a course in nursing premature babies and went to work in Dorset. Later, I gained extra qualifications in Health Visiting and District Nursing.

Carmen left Health Visting in 1967 to become a Community Relations Officer in Bristol. She is now Senior CRO there and was awarded the MBE in January 1983.

Mrs Eugene: I was born in Dominica and came to England in October 1960 on board the *Askyana*. I went to live with my brother in Bristol. He had been here for a year after hearing that building workers were needed in Britain.

When I arrived I was very impressed with the huge city buildings and also with snow which I had not seen before. It was quite easy to come over: it seemed to be the thing to do at that time to look for a job.

I got married in 1962 to a carpenter who had also come from Dominica. Mostly the people from the different Caribbean islands tend to stick together. Since I had my family I have had various jobs working in shops and in a hospital. At the moment I work in an old people's home.

My daughters, Judy, Sherry and Paula, were born here but are proud of their Dominican roots. Sherry appears on HTV as a sign language interpreter for the deaf, and Paula is training to be a nurse.

For many black people, coming to live here has not always brought happiness. Racial **prejudice**, lowly-paid jobs, unemployment and poor housing were, and still are, a problem. This prejudice will be looked at in 'The Opposition' on Page 40.

Things to do

1 In your own words, explain why
  a) the first black people were brought to this country.
  b) their numbers fell in the 19th century.
  c) numbers began to increase in the 1950s.
2 What did, or do, each of the following do for a living in this country:
Sherry Eugene, Ignatius Sancho, Scipio Africanus, Bill Richmond, Mr Eugene?

27

c) Asian Settlers

When these members of the 8th Punjab Pipe Band were celebrating the end of the Second World War in Birmingham in May 1945, the subcontinent of India was still ruled by Britain. Two years later, in August 1947, it became independent. The state of Pakistan was also created at this time.

Immigration into Britain from India, Pakistan and from Asian communities in Africa and the West Indies did not start until a few years after independence. But what made Asian people choose to come to Britain rather than live in the newly independent countries? Dr Bikhu Parekh of the University of Hull suggests that there were three main reasons:

> Asian immigrants came to Britain for a variety of reasons. . . . Some had tied themselves too closely to British rule, and could not survive its disappearance. . . . Some others had acquired a love of the British way of life and felt that they would be happier in Britain than in their own countries. . . . Many, however, immigrated because . . . they had developed a tradition of migration in search of better prospects.

Most of the early **immigrants** did not expect to spend all their lives in Britain. They planned to work and save enough money to bring their families over (if they had come on their own as many did) before returning to their own countries. In the 1950s and 1960s Britain encouraged workers to come. However, many found that it took them much longer to save than they had thought as wages were low. **Immigration** laws also delayed the arrival of their families.

The second generation of Asian immigrants either came to join their husbands and fathers or were born in this country. Many Asian children know no other home than Britain and do not wish to return to India or Pakistan like their parents. For them, brought up and educated in Britain, their future lies in this country.

The 8th Punjab Pipe Band in Birmingham

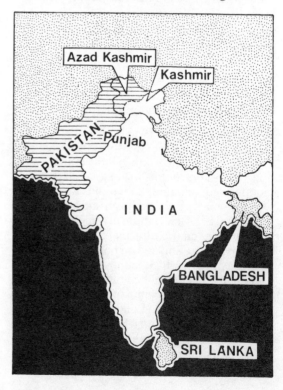

Yasin Khan on his wedding day

Yasin Khan came to Britain when he was 18 to join his father who had come some years before. He describes why and how they both came to settle here:

I was born in 1959 in a small village called Dingle in the Mirpur district of Azad Kashmir which is north of Pakistan. Like others in my village my parents were poor. My father was a farmer but everybody in our family used to work in the fields to try and grow enough to eat. This was almost impossible because during the summer months there was hardly any rain.

My father decided that there was no future in farming so he made up his mind to go abroad in search of a job. It took him several months to get a passport, visa and work permit before he came to Britain in 1960.

When he arrived he stayed with relatives in Coventry. He got a job working for Dunlop Ltd, and later moved to Birmingham where he still works in a paper mill. He worked hard and sent money to us. After about four and a half years he came back to Azad Kashmir for a while to see us. While he was there he built us a better house to live in.

In 1975 I left school and went to college. My relatives often told me stories about Britain and its people which interested me. I wrote to my father saying that I would like to come to Britain. He sent me the necessary sponsor letter and I applied for a visa to the British Embassy in Islamabad in Pakistan. It took me a year and a half to get it!

I came to Britain in May 1977 with my mother and youngest sister. When we landed at Heathrow Airport and we got out of the 'plane I felt cold although it was summer. I felt that I had come to a new world where everything looked strange to me – white people, a new language which I couldn't understand, new culture, new fashions and many other things. I came from a small village where we didn't have houses like here, nor electricity, gas, telephones, paved roads or television.

I went to evening classes to improve my English, and after a year and a half got a job as a capstan lathe operator. At first I was shy about speaking to my workmates because I wasn't too good at understanding English and I thought I might say something wrong, but all the staff and workers were nice. I left that job to go to college where I studied mainly Maths and English. In June 1982 I got married to a British-born Asian girl and we are now living with my parents.

Things to do

1 Look at the reasons Dr Parekh gives for Asian **immigration** on Page 28. Which of them explains why Yasin's father decided to come to Britain?
2 What did Yasin need before he got permission to come to Britain? Do you think that it was easy or hard for him to join his father?
3 Imagine that you are planning to go and live in a foreign country like Yasin. Write a letter to a relative or friend there. What sort of things are you going to ask about?

5 The Refugees

Nobody chooses to become a refugee: it is something that they are forced to do. Refugees are people who have to leave their own homes and often their own countries to escape from something.

The news today is often full of stories of refugees escaping from wars, **persecution** or natural disasters such as earthquakes, floods or **famine**. We sometimes hear in the news of people seeking **political asylum** in a foreign country. These people do not like what is happening in their own land or they are in danger there – they are refugees as well.

These pictures are of some famous people who became political refugees in the past. Each of them escaped from their own country because they were not safe there and came to live in Britain for a time. In this chapter we shall look at some groups of refugees who came to Britain to find out when and why they came and what they contributed to British society.

LOUIS PHILIPPE — King of the French 1848

PRINCE METTERNICH — Chancellor of the Austrian Empire 1848

GIUSEPPE MAZZINI — Italian nationalist and revolutionary 1837

KARL MARX — German writer 1849

EUGÉNIE — Empress of France 1870

LENIN — Russian revolutionary 1903

a) The Huguenots

The Huguenots were French Protestants. During the 16th and 17th centuries Protestants living in Roman Catholic countries in Europe were often attacked because of their religious beliefs.

In 1567 Dutch Protestants came under attack and many fled to England which, under Queen Elizabeth I, was a Protestant country. Five years later large numbers of French Protestant refugees were forced to follow their example. In 1572 over 50 000 Huguenots were killed in France in the Massacre of St Bartholomew's Eve. The shortest route to safety was across the English Channel.

In 1598 the French king issued the Edict of Nantes which allowed the Huguenots to worship freely, and for nearly a hundred years they were free from attack. However, in 1685 King Louis XVI cancelled the Edict and attacks on the Huguenots began again. Once more the refugees began to escape across the Channel.

It is thought that up to 100 000 Huguenots fled to Britain although many moved on to live in Holland and America. Those who stayed settled down and intermarried with the British. Many changed their names from French to English so that Leroys became Kings and Lejeunes became Youngs.

Britain was fortunate to have them living here. Most of them were educated, skilled workers who made a major contribution to the economy. It was their skills that developed silk weaving, hat making, glass engraving and the manufacture of quality paper. They introduced the making of fine cloths like velvets, brocades, satin and lace. They made improvements in the sail making, linen and leather industries. Many of them served in the British army.

Some of the Huguenots and their descendants became famous. Thomas Savery invented one of the first steam-engines in 1698. Lewis Paul built a spinning machine in the 1730s (which Richard Arkwright was to improve to make his 'Water Frame'). David Garrick, the actor, and Cardinal Newman both had Huguenot **ancestors**. Augustin Courtauld's descendants founded the textile firm which still bears his name, and John Dolland made major improvements in the manufacture of microscopes and telescopes. You may have a Dolland microscope at your school or know somebody who has a pair of Dolland binoculars.

Huguenots landing at Dover in 1685

Things to do

Copy this square of letters into your book and see how many Huguenot names and industries you can spot in it. There are twelve to find.

```
C D F N R G H N Q K
E O K S I L K J O M
M L U O S A I L S R
P L G R U S P H B Z
S A H A T S I P R A
T N P Q W A L A O I
X D J E B V U U C S
C Y C E R E Z L A V
F A V G D R P X D Q
L I N E N Y W B E L
```

b) The Irish

In the first half of the 19th century most of the ordinary people in Ireland relied on the potato for their main food. They grew other crops but sold them to pay the rents on their farms or smallholdings. In 1845 the potato crop was hit by a disease which caused the potato to rot to a stinking pulp. The next year the disease spread more widely. It did not disappear until 1851. These were the years of the Great **Famine**: of starvation, disease and death.

For centuries before, there had been a small but steady stream of Irish people coming across the Irish Sea to look for work and better living conditions. Many had settled in London, Manchester and the ports of Glasgow and Liverpool. When the **Famine** struck, this stream became a flood. The reason for their coming was simple – if they had not come they would have died.

What were the conditions they had left behind like? A magistrate called Nicholas Cummins visited the village of Skibbereen in County Cork in 1846. He wrote this about what he saw:

> I entered some of the hovels . . . and the scenes which presented themselves were such as no tongue or pen can convey the slightest idea of. In the first, six famished and ghastly skeletons, to all appearances dead, were huddled in a corner on some filthy straw, their sole covering which seemed a ragged horsecloth, their wretched legs hanging about, naked above the knees. I approached with horror, and found by a low moaning they were alive – they were in fever, four children, a woman and what had once been a man. . . . The same morning the police opened a house on the adjoining lands, which was observed shut for many days, and two dead corpses were found, lying upon the mud floor, half devoured [eaten] by rats.

Pictures like this from the *Illustrated London News* showed people what the famine was like

Another victim of the famine

Almost a million people in Ireland died during the **Famine**. Millions more **emigrated** to escape. They went to America, Canada and other parts of Britain. Although Ireland was still part of the United Kingdom at that time, these Irish refugees were looked upon by many people as foreigners. The English in particular complained about their living habits but often spoke highly of them as workers. In 1836 a Birmingham employer had said this of Irish workers:

> The Irish labourers will work at any time. . . . I consider them very valuable labourers, and we could not do without them. By treating them kindly, they will do anything for you. . . . An Englishman could not do the work they do. When you push them they have a willingness to oblige which the English have not; they would die under anything before they would be beat; they would go at hard work till they drop before a man would excel them . . .

In the middle of the 19th century there was plenty of work for them to do. Many became 'navvies' and helped to build the railways, canals and roads which British industry needed. They worked on the

Church Lane, St Giles, London, where many Irish **immigrants** lived

docks, on building sites, joined the armed forces and became street traders. Their contribution to the Industrial Revolution in this country was vital.

Navvies at work on the Manchester Ship Canal

Things to do
1 Which one of the following sentences do you think explains why there was so much starvation and hardship in Ireland between 1845 and 1851?
   a) The Irish people only grew potatoes and when this crop failed they had no food.
   b) There was plenty of food in Ireland but the ordinary people could not afford to buy it.
   c) The Irish people had to sell their other crops to pay their rents and so had to rely on the potato even when the crop failed.
2 Imagine that you are a visitor present at the scene in the picture at the foot of the opposite page. Write down what you see and your feelings about it.
3 What contribution did the Irish workers make when they came across to England?
4 What is unusual about one of the navvies in the picture above? Describe how the appearance of these men differs from that of modern building workers.

c) The East European Jews

My father came from Poland . . . What brought him over from Poland was the **pogroms** against the Jews. It was terrible. He was one of 13 children, and their mother and father did their best to get all their children away, knowing they'd probably never see them again. . . .

My father came to England, and after that his brothers and sister went to America and Canada. His father died in Poland, but his mother came away eventually.

Mr Lesser was born in Birmingham in 1912. It is his father whom he remembers in this passage. He was one of the thousands of East European Jews who fled from Russia and Poland at the end of the 19th century.

In 1881 Tsar Alexander II, the Russian Emperor, was killed when a bomb was thrown at him. A member of the group who had planned the attack was a Jewish girl called Hesia Helfman. The Russian authorities used this as an excuse to attack the Jews in the Russian Empire. Poland was part of this empire at that time.

The Russian Jews had been treated badly by the Russian Christians for a long time. They had to live in special areas and there were special laws for them. After 1881 things got even worse. The areas where

EUROPE, POLAND AND RUSSIA, 1881

An attack on a Russian Jew

34

they were able to live were made even smaller. Attacks on Jews in Eastern Europe became more common and many were killed. The picture on page 34 shows the sort of treatment that many Jews were given. It was painted at the end of the 19th century.

Mr Lesser remembers talking to his father about what it was like to live in Poland:

I remember he [his father] had a very big cyst [a sore] on the back of his neck, and I said to him one day, 'What caused that?' . . . my father was sitting on a log one day, he was only a boy of about 10, and at the time it [Poland] was under Russian rule. The Cossacks [Russian cavalry] rode through the village, just for devilment, lashing out with their long whips . . . and that whipping caused this cyst.

Mr Lesser's father

Over a million Jews fled from the **pogroms**. Many went to America but about 100 000 chose to settle in Britain between 1881 and 1914. Some had money but most were working class and poor and had left nearly all their belongings behind. Very few could speak any English. Most spoke Yiddish.

When they got off the boats they made their way to those cities which already had Jewish communities such as London, Manchester and Leeds. There they knew they would find the synagogues and **kosher** butchers they needed and people who spoke their language.

The British Jews welcomed the refugees but they were worried about what the rest of the population would think of the new arrivals. They set about trying to make the refugees as British as possible as soon as possible. They encouraged them to dress in the British way and to learn English. They tried to find them jobs, decent houses and schools.

Many of the British Jews who were here before the end of the 19th century had their own businesses. They gave jobs to the refugees before they set up on their own. Mr Lesser's father worked for an uncle until he got married and opened his own shop. The refugees became tailors, makers of boots and shoes, furniture and cigarettes. They worked long hours for low wages in places called 'sweat shops' because of the poor conditions. Most of the things they made were cheap: the sort of things ordinary people could afford, although quite a few became jewellers. Jewish tailors were some of the first to make full use of the sewing-machine which had been invented earlier in the century.

Mr Lesser's shop in 1912

Things to do

1 In your own words, explain when and why so many Jews left Eastern Europe at the end of the 19th century.
2 Look at the picture on the opposite page. Do you think the artist meant you to feel sorry for the Jewish victim or not? Could anybody stop what is happening? Are they likely to? Give reasons for your answer.

d) The Ugandan Asians

In January 1971 President Obote of Uganda was overthrown by the commander of the army. This man was Major General Idi Amin. He then became the new president.

President Idi Amin

Ugandan refugees at Stansted airport

Uganda had been a British colony until 1962 when it became independent. In 1971 it was still part of the Commonwealth and many Ugandans were British citizens: they still had British passports. Many of the factories, businesses and shops in Uganda were run by Asians. President Amin thought that they should be run by black Ugandans.

On 4 August 1972 President Amin said that all Asians who had British passports must leave Uganda within 90 days. This meant that 50 000 people were suddenly told that their own country no longer wanted them. But where were they to go?

Many of them looked to this country for help because they were British citizens. The British Government agreed to take them but it did not know how many people would come. It set up the Uganda Resettlement Board (URB) to deal with the refugees and began to make plans for an air-lift to bring them here. Meanwhile, the URB set up 16 temporary camps (usually old military bases) to house the newcomers.

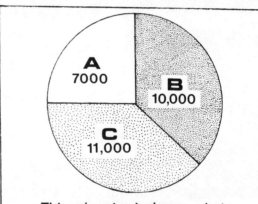

This pie-chart shows what happened to the refugees in Britain. Group A had places to go to as soon as they arrived. Group B found their own places to live after arriving. The URB found homes for Group C after they had left the camps.

The air-lift began on 18 September and ended on 7 November 1972. It brought about 28 000 people to Britain. Only those with British passports and their dependants (wives and children) were allowed here at first. This meant that some families were split up with some members having to remain in Uganda.

What you have read so far are the facts about what happened, but what was it like for the people who were expelled from Uganda? This is what one family remembers:

Mr Abdulhusein Dungarwalla and his wife and two children lived in Kampala, the capital of Uganda, where he owned a shop. His wife came from a Ugandan Asian family but he had come from Bombay in India. His son was 17 and his daughter was 15 at the time.

> The first time I heard about what was to happen was when the President [Amin] spoke on the radio. It was a surprise. After that it was in the papers and on TV.

He remembered how he lost his shop.

> One day some soldiers came. They told me I had a day to shut my shop. After that I had to lock up and give them the key. I took some things with me to my house but I had to leave almost everything behind. They took it all. I never got any money for my shop. At the time soldiers were smashing up the shops and houses of Asians.

His son Ibrahim was abroad in India studying when he heard the news.

> At first I thought it was a joke. The Asian people had deep roots in Uganda. They didn't believe that the President would do it. After a while I realised it was going to happen – I started to panic! I had a return air ticket and was going to use it, but my dad told me to stay where I was, where I was safe.

Mrs Dungarwalla had a British passport and so she was able to fly to Britain in the air-lift.

> I went with my daughter. All we had were suitcases; we couldn't bring anything else. When we got here we were sent to a camp at Eccleshall in Staffordshire. It was a military camp I think. It wasn't bad: we were in proper houses and a lot of people helped us. After a week my daughter started school. We were at the camp for nearly three months and then we were moved to Winsford in Cheshire. Later, we came here to Birmingham to live. This is our home now. We like it here. We wouldn't go back [to Uganda].

Mr Dungarwalla had to wait before he came. He had a Ugandan passport. He joined his wife and daughter in 1973. Ibrahim came here from his studies in India.

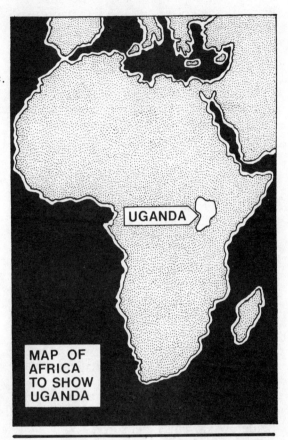

UGANDA

MAP OF AFRICA TO SHOW UGANDA

Things to do

1 Why could Mr Dungarwalla not go with his wife and daughter to Britain straight away?
2 If you had to leave this country for good and could only take two suitcases with you, what would you pack in them?
3 What do you think needed to be done for the refugees as soon as they arrived in this country? Arrange this list in order of priority and explain the reason for your decisions. You can add to the list.
   houses, medical help, food, clothing, schools for children, jobs for adults

The refugees we have read about so far were escaping from famine and religious or racial persecution. War is another reason why people are forced to leave their homes and countries. Two groups of people who came to Britain in recent years because of wars are the Poles and the Vietnamese 'Boat People'.

e) The Poles

On 3 September 1939, Britain and France declared war on Germany because Adolf Hitler refused to stop his invasion of Poland. This was the start of the Second World War.

Before he ordered his troops to invade Poland, Hitler made an agreement with Stalin, the Russian leader. In this Nazi-Soviet Pact of August 1939, they agreed not to fight each other and to divide Poland between them. In June 1941 Hitler broke this agreement by invading Russia.

When their country was invaded, the Poles fought bravely but they were no match for the German 'blitzkrieg' attack. The Polish government and many airmen and others escaped to Britain where they were able to continue the fight against Nazi Germany.

One of the Poles who was affected by the Nazi-Soviet Pact and the war is Mrs Zyta Szulejewska. This is her story:

> After the Nazi-Soviet Pact, my family and I were put into trucks by the Russians and driven away from our home near Lvov in Eastern Poland. I was just six when they took us to a labour camp in Siberia in 1940. We all had to work very hard, even my mother who was pregnant, and were hardly given anything to eat. Many people died, especially the small children. Even the guards had little food or comfort.
>
> When Hitler invaded Russia in 1941 we were released. Somebody simply came and said that all the Poles in our camp could go. But where were we to go? Eventually, in rags and with our heads shaved to prevent lice, we were taken to Krasnowock near the Caspian

Sea where we were given food and clothing. The men who could fight were trained and sent to join General Montgomery and the British in North Africa. The rest of us were sent to any friendly country that would take us.

We went at first to Persia [now Iran] and then to Lebanon in 1944. We all dreamed of returning home to Poland but then we heard what had happened at the meeting at Yalta. We were shocked when we learned that at that meeting Churchill, Roosevelt and Stalin had agreed that Russia should be given part of Poland after the war. Our home was in that part!

We were told that we could go back home but we were afraid that the Russians would send us to Siberia again. Many other Poles felt the same. We chose to go to Britain where lots of our people had been living while they were fighting against Germany. We arrived by ship in Liverpool in February 1948 and were sent to camps in Staffordshire and then Devon.

I went to schools in Cheltenham and Newton Abbot before going to Bristol University in 1954 where I studied History. While I was there I went to a Polish reunion in London where I met my husband.

Polish airmen in Britain in 1945

At the end of the war in 1945 there were about 250 000 Poles in Britain. Many went back to Poland or crossed the Atlantic to find new homes, but over 100 000 chose to remain here. In time many were joined by their families.

To help them to make a start in this country the Polish Resettlement Corps was set up in 1947. It helped the ex-servicemen to find civilian jobs and homes and schools for their families.

f) The Vietnamese 'Boat People'

The Vietnam War ended for the Americans in 1975 when communist North Vietnamese troops drove them out of Saigon, the capital of South Vietnam. However, the fighting which had also involved Laos and Cambodia did not end then. Communist forces took over those countries as well causing thousands of people to become refugees. More began to flee when war broke out between Vietnam and Cambodia in 1978.

By road and by sea the refugees tried to escape from the fighting or from the **persecution** of their new governments. The 'Boat People' crowded on to almost anything that would float and set sail across the South China Sea. Disease, starvation,

storms and attacks by pirates killed thousands of them. Those who managed to reach the safety of a foreign land or were picked up by passing ships faced another problem – where were they to go now? Who would offer them a home?

An international conference was held in Geneva in Switzerland in July 1979 to try to find an answer to this problem. Those lands where the refugees had first arrived, either by road or sea, were unwilling or unable to accept them all and wanted other countries to take their 'share'. Britain was one of the countries that agreed to offer a new home to some of the 'Boat People'. Over 10 000 have since come here to start new lives.

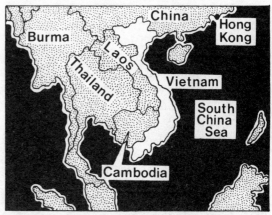

Vietnamese boat people on the South China Sea

Things to do

1 Use an atlas to trace or copy a map of Europe and the Middle East. On the map mark the route Zyta took from her home in Poland to the time she arrived in this country.

2 Here are two questions for you to discuss in your class. You could divide yourselves into smaller groups or have a class discussion.

   a) Why do you think that Vietnam's neighbours were 'unwilling or unable' to accept the 'Boat People'?

   b) Why have many refugees chosen to remain in Britain even though it later became safe for them to return to their original countries?

6 The Opposition

It is easy to understand why people living in Britain opposed the coming of the conquerors: they were defending their country against attack by armed invaders. However, even those people who came here peacefully and in much smaller numbers met with opposition. Sometimes this opposition was violent.

In 1190 a baron called Richard Malebysse attacked a Jewish family in their home in York. Like other local nobles he owed money to Jewish moneylenders. The violence spread and, afraid for their lives, the rest of the Jewish community in the city shut themselves in the wooden keep of the castle (Clifford's Tower now stands on the spot). A mob surrounded the keep and the Jewish men, women and children inside killed themselves rather than be torn to pieces.

On 'Evil May Day' in 1517 a London mob ran through the streets attacking foreign merchants and their property. A rumour, based on a church sermon, had spread that foreigners were to be killed to protect native English people. Dislike of the many wealthy foreign merchants meant that many people were willing to take part. The rioting did not last for long and the ringleaders were hanged.

The strange cry of 'No Jews; no wooden shoes' was heard in London in 1753. Parliament that year passed an act to say that Jewish **immigrants'** children born in Britain could be given British citizenship. This led to protests, not only against Jews but also against other 'foreigners'. The 'wooden shoes' referred to the clogs worn by the Huguenots who had been welcomed when they first arrived as refugees.

Clifford's Tower, York

In 1919 there were several attacks on black people in some British cities. White servicemen returning from the First World War were angry that black people had been given jobs while they were unemployed, even though many black people had fought in the war. *The Times* of 11 June 1919 described what took place in Liverpool:

> The police have issued a warning that severe measures will be taken against anyone attempting to wreck property or to attack members of the coloured community, many of whom are inoffensive and have given distinguished service during the war. Scores of coloured men and women, some of them with their families, have gone to the local police headquarters asking for protection, and last evening over 60 of them were taken into the care of the police.

In August 1958 fighting broke out between groups of black and white people in Nottingham following attacks on black people there. Newspapers, radio and television reported the violence and this led to more trouble in parts of London. In the Notting Hill area, gangs of white youths attacked black people and threw bricks and petrol bombs at their homes. More recently, tension between white and black people resulted in outbreaks of violence.

Why has there always been opposition to **immigrants** in this country? Some people believe that it is something new and yet almost every group of new arrivals here has met with suspicion, dislike and **prejudice**, if not actual violence.

Today **immigrants** from the Caribbean and the Indian sub-continent still meet with opposition. In addition, their colour identifies them, in many people's eyes, as being 'foreign'. Even those who were born in Britain meet with this sort of **prejudice**.

A great deal of this **prejudice** is based on misunderstanding and fear: fear about numbers and competition for jobs and houses as well as the different life-styles of black people. Recent official statistics show that these fears are unjustified. The following facts, published by the Commission for Racial Equality in 1982, are based on these statistics.

FACT: The latest estimate (mid 1980) of the size of the black population is 2.1 million – 3.9% of the total population. In 1974 nearly 40% of the black people had been born in Great Britain.

FACT: Since 1964 more people have left the U.K. each year than entered. In 1980, 174,000 people came to live in Britain and 229,000 left.

FACT: Urban decay has existed in this country since the Industrial Revolution. Bad housing conditions were here long before black immigrants. In the areas where 70% of black people live, eight out of ten people are white.

FACT: Most families from the Asian and West Indian Communities have sought owner occupation as a solution to their housing problems. 76% of Asians and 50% of West Indians are owner-occupiers compared with 54% of the overall population. As far as council housing is concerned, 4% of Asians and 26% of West Indians live in council house accommodation, compared with about 30% of the population as a whole.

FACT: As unemployment rises, unemployment among ethnic minority workers rises faster than general unemployment.

Racial discrimination makes it harder for a black man than for a white man to get a job.

Things to do
Discuss with your teacher the possible reasons for the opposition described on these two pages. How truthful or reasonable do you think these reasons are (look at the FACTS)?

The traditional dislike of the life-styles of new arrivals and the fear that they would lower wages or put people out of work reached a peak at the end of the 19th century. One result of the arrival of refugees from Eastern Europe at that time was the formation of organisations whose aim was to limit or stop **immigration**.

One of these was the British Brothers' League which was set up in 1901. It was active until 1905 and claimed to have 20 000 members, although fewer than 2000 ever paid a subscription. Like the Londoners' League of 1901, it had a mainly working class membership and wanted Parliament to pass anti-immigration laws.

a) The Fascists

Arnold Leese was a veterinary surgeon who was born in Lytham in Lancashire in 1878. He believed that **immigration** should be stopped. He also believed that the white 'Aryan' race of Northern Europe was superior to all other races in the world.

He had been a member of The British Fascists, an organisation which had been founded in 1923 as a copy of Mussolini's Italian 'fascisti'. He left in 1928 to set up the Imperial Fascist League. Neither of these two groups ever had much support or influence but their ideas were taken up by a man who was to hit the headlines.

His name was Oswald Mosley and he had been an MP for both the Conservative and Labour Parties. In 1932 he founded the British Union of Fascists (BUF) and gave its members a uniform of black shirts to wear. At meetings the 'blackshirts' used the same salute as the Nazis in Germany. Mosley claimed that the Jews in Britain were unpatriotic and should be deported.

On 4 October 1936 the BUF organised a march through the East End of London. They planned to pass through an area where many Jewish people lived. Barricades were put up to stop them and fighting broke out. The 'Battle of Cable Street', as this was called, led to Parliament

passing the Public Order Act of November 1936. This said that the authorities could ban the wearing of uniforms for political purposes and the police could ban processions for up to three months if they got the permission of the Home Secretary. This act is still used today.

Oswald Moseley addressing a fascist meeting in 1936

The 'Battle' of Cable Street

The BUF did not survive the Second World War of 1939-1945. People in Britain would not support fascists at home while they were fighting fascists abroad and the government took steps against the organisation and against Mosley. However, the beliefs of the fascists have never completely disappeared and opposition to the Jews and non-white **immigration** is still carried on by some groups today.

b) The Law and Immigration

Until the 20th century, Britain had provided a home for people who had to leave their own countries. Although these people were often disliked as described earlier in this section, the door to settlement here had always been kept open for them. However, throughout this century that door has gradually been closed more and more by a series of Acts of Parliament restricting **immigration**. These are some of the main acts.

Aliens Act, 1905
Only **immigrants** with 'visible means of support' were to be allowed to enter Britain at 14 ports where **immigration** officials could turn people away. In 1906 just under 500 were refused entry.

Aliens Restriction Acts, 1914 and 1919
Aliens could again be refused entry and those already here could be deported if the Home Secretary thought it was 'in the public good'. People who were not Commonwealth citizens holding British passports had to obtain a work permit if they wanted to stay longer than three months. They also had to register with the police.

British Nationality Act, 1948
This confirmed the right of British passport holders from throughout the Commonwealth to enter Britain freely with their families and live and work here.

Commonwealth Immigrants Act, 1962
This act limited the right of Commonwealth people with British passports to live and work in Britain. **Immigrants** had to obtain an employment voucher before they came. Over the next ten years the number of vouchers issued was decreased.

Commonwealth Immigrants Act, 1968
Immigration to Britain was restricted to those people who could prove that their parents or grandparents were born here.

Immigration Act, 1971
Only people born in Britain or whose parents were born in Britain had a right to live here. Others had to obtain a work permit. Male work permit holders could bring their wives and children, but female work permit holders could not bring their husbands and children.

British Nationality Act, 1981
'An Act to make fresh provision about citizenship and nationality, and so amend the Immigration Act of 1971 as regards the right of abode in the United Kingdom.'

This Act set out different types of British citizenship and nationality. Not all of them give a person the right to live and work in Britain.

Things to do
1 How did the views of the Fascists differ from those of previous opponents of immigration?
2 Some people today say that it is too easy for immigrants to come to live and work in Britain. From what you have read, say whether you agree or disagree with them and why.
3 With the rest of the class or in groups, discuss how you think minority groups feel about this opposition. Could, or should, they do anything about it?

---

7 The Enrichment of Britain

We have seen that for hundreds of years people from many different countries have been coming to live and work in Britain. As well as helping to create our nation's wealth, they have fought for their new country in several wars.

Other groups have arrived in Britain in recent years: the Europeans recruited after the Second World War as European Voluntary Workers, Chinese from Hong Kong, Cypriots, Greeks, Italians and many, many more. These people brought with them their own customs and cultures to add to those they found in this country.

It is no wonder that Britain is such a rich and varied nation culturally. In this section we shall be looking at just a few of the ways in which the different groups of people have contributed to our way of life today.

a) Festivals

Fairy stories and legends are not the only places where dragons can be found in Britain! The Chinese communities in this country celebrate their New Year during the first week of February. Accompanied by drums and cymbals, men in dragon costumes dance through the streets to keep away evil spirits. This is just one of the many festivals brought to Britain. Here are some others:

Christmas – the day in December when Christians celebrate the birth of Christ was also the last day of the Roman festival of 'Saturnalia': a time of feasting and merry-making.

Yom Kippur – the Jews' holiest day: the 'Day of Atonement'.

Holi – the Hindus' festival of colours, when they play tricks and throw coloured powder and water at each other.

Baisakhi – an important festival for the Sikhs, which is also the time of their New Year.

Id-Ul-Fitr – marks the end of fasting during Ramadan for Moslems. It is a time when they hold parties and give presents.

Samain – was the old Celtic festival on 1st November when ghosts and spirits wandered through the land. We still celebrate Halloween at this time.

Dragon dance

b) Food

This is now a familiar sight in many British high streets and yet it is a fairly new one. Today we take Indian and Chinese food for granted. Not many years ago very few people in this country had ever tasted them!

Changes in our eating habits have been brought about not only by the fact that more people go abroad for their holidays and try foreign foods, but also because of the foods brought here by immigrants. Many of you will have tasted a curry, Italian spaghetti and pizza, Greek kebabs and other foods. The next time you go into a supermarket, see how many foreign foods you can see for sale on the shelves.

Can you tell in which sort of restaurant you would expect to be able to enjoy these dishes: Tandoori chicken, Taramasalata, sweet and sour pork, Cannelloni?

c) Language

As well as people, new words have always been arriving in this country. The English language has changed a great deal since the days of the Anglo-Saxons. This is what their English looked like. It comes from the Saxon peom *Beowulf*.

> Fortham Offa waes geofum ond guthum, garcene man wide geweorthod; wisdome heold ethel sinne.

Translated, this means 'Best of men the wide world over, Offa was a great warrior who ruled his kingdom wisely and was famous for his victories and his generosity'.

The familiar words in the speech bubbles are all foreign additions to English. Can you tell which of these languages they came from originally:

French   Yiddish   Sanskrit   Arabic
Hindi   Dutch   American Indian
Spanish   Gaelic

d) Music

One of the most famous people to come to live in this country was the composer, George Frederick Handel (1685-1759). He was born in Germany but spent most of his working life in England. Among his best-known works are the 'Messiah' and the 'Water Music', which was composed for King George I.

In our own time, popular as well as classical music has been influenced by people who have come to live and work in Britain and who have brought their own musical traditions with them. Perhaps the most influential of contributions this century has been that of black musicians.

Jazz and rock both have their roots in the music of the black people of America. Recently, musical styles from the West Indies have been brought across the Atlantic. In the 1950s came calypso, in the 1960s ska, and in recent years reggae.

Asian music has never enjoyed the same widespread popularity in this country, but it has influenced several bands. Perhaps the most famous of these, the Beatles, used eastern instruments such as the sitar on albums such as 'Revolver' in 1966 and 'Sgt Pepper's Lonely Hearts Club Band' in 1967.

George Frederick Handel

e) Dress

Most of the people who have come to this country in the past have chosen to wear the same sort of everyday clothes as the rest of the population. However, there are some exceptions and these help to add variety to dress in Britain.

Bob Marley, who was a major influence on reggae music in Britain

Cappel

Turban

Tam

For some people, what they wear is influenced by their religious beliefs. The three types of head covering shown on page 46 are examples of this. The Jewish boy wears a 'cappel' or small skullcap. He wears this when he prays, but some Jewish men wear the cappel all the time.

You may have seen some black men and boys wearing a knitted woollen hat, or tam. Rastafarians believe that they should not cut their hair and so they grow it into long 'dreadlocks' which they often cover with these hats.

Baptised Sikhs, too, believe that they should not cut their hair. They tie it up into a knot on the top of their heads. The turban is wrapped and fastened round the head to cover the hair.

Moslem women may not show their bare arms or legs and so wear their traditional clothes to cover them. In some countries they cover their faces in public as well, but this does not happen very often in Britain.

The picture below shows a woman wearing a sari. This is a long piece of fine material (often silk) which is wound round the body to make a long, loose-fitting dress. Many Moslem schoolgirls wear normal school uniform but with long trousers underneath their dresses. The traditional trousers, which are slightly gathered at the ankles, are called 'shalwar'.

Sari

Moslem girl

Things to do

1 Copy this word grid into your exercise book. Find the words from this section to match the descriptions and fit them into the squares. The descriptions are not in the same order as the word grid.

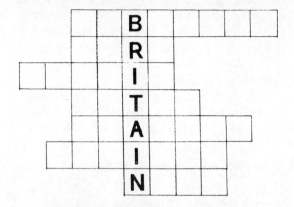

A   A Spanish flavour.
B   Month of the dragon.
C   One of the Sergeant's instruments.
D   Yiddish 'grub'.
E   Girls' trousers.
F   When Celtic ghosts are seen.
G   'Nothing' from Arabic.

2 Try designing and making your own Chinese dragon, either as a model or a collage picture. Paint it in bright colours.
3 Find out how people celebrate the festivals mentioned in this section. Is any special food eaten or are special clothes worn during them?
4 Make a display in your classroom of popular foreign foods eaten in this country. You could collect empty packets and the labels off tins to help you.
5 Can somebody in your class or school show you how to fasten a sari or a turban? It not, try to find out for yourself from a book in your school or local library.

Suggestions for Further Work

a) Further reading

G. Ashworth, *The Boat People* (Quartermaine House, 1979)

N. File and C. Power, *Black Settlers in Britain 1555-1958* (Heinemann, 1981)

C. Nicholson, *Strangers to England* (Wayland 1974)

C. Roth, *A History of the Jews in Britain* (Clarendon Press, Oxford, 1964)

F. M. Wilson, *They Came as Strangers* (Hamish Hamilton, 1959)

The Commission for Racial Equality, 10/12 Allington Street, London SW1E 5EH, will send a list of its publications, many of which are free.

b) Project work in small groups

Here are some suggestions. Use your school and local libraries for information.

1 Make folders of written work and pictures about some of the groups of people you have read about in this book. Find out what life was like in the countries they came from and what their life here was/is like.

2 Find out about the history of the city, town or village where you live. Is there any evidence in your area of the different groups of people who have come to Britain?

3 Make a calendar of holidays and festivals held by different groups in Britain. Find out why and how they first started.

4 Look up the meanings of the first names and surnames of people in your class. Find out where the names come from. There are special books that tell you this.

5 Do you know somebody whose family came to Britain from another country? If so, they might be willing to tell you their story. You could either write it down or record it.

c) Classroom wall displays

1 Make a large map of the world and fix it to the wall or display board. Mark on it (using labels or small flags fastened to pins) where the grandparents of everybody in your class (or even year group) were born.

2 Make a time chart by sticking sheets of paper together to make a long strip and divide it into centuries (start at 600 BC). Show on it when the different groups of people you have learned about in this book came here, as well as what you think are important dates in History.

d) Class discussion

Here are some ideas for you to discuss with your class and teacher.

What do *you* think about immigration to this country? Have these ideas been changed at all by what you have read in this book? Should we encourage or discourage immigration to Britain? Give reasons for your opinion.

Should we expect immigrants to give up their own customs and traditions when they come to live here? How much would *you* change *your* way of life if you went to live abroad?

Glossary

alien	a foreigner or stranger
ancestor	a member of the family who died a long time ago
archaeologist	somebody who studies the past by looking at things people left behind
destitute	without food or shelter
emigrate	to go to live in another country
famine	a serious shortage of food
immigrant	a person who comes to live in a different country
immigration	coming to live in a different country
inscription	something that is written on a building or object
kosher	food prepared according to Jewish law
persecution	organised ill-treatment, usually of a religious or political group
to plunder	to steal
pogrom	organised attacks on Russian Jews
political asylum	shelter given to somebody escaping from his/her own country
prejudice	(here) disliking people because of their race or religion